The Danger Zones

The Top 5 Risk Areas Employers Don't Realize Can Put Them Out of Business (And What To Do About Them!)

Brett Trembly

Here's What's Inside...

Message from the Author

There's a common misconception that once you have a good idea, owning a business is easy, and the money rolls in. When speaking to and counseling thousands of entrepreneurs over the years, the energy and excitement always exceed the details. Of course, entrepreneurs, employers, and managers know that running a successful business isn't easy—but it *could* be, and it *should* be. With the proper legal, financial, and operational guidance, owning a business can be fun again.

Our business, the Trembly Law Firm, has had over fifty percent growth for seven straight years and was recently named to the prestigious Inc. 5000 list. Starting from a one-person, do-everything operation in late 2011, we have ten attorneys and 25 employees, and despite COVID-19, we don't see the growth slowing down any time soon.

With every great hire we make, we not only ensure each team member fits our core values, but we also implement structured training programs to set them up for success. By implementing an annual business plan and then faithfully executing our proven system for success, we continue to help more and more clients while other business law firms stagnate.

In other words, we make sure our own business is secure, protected, and running like a well-oiled machine, all prerequisites before we can help our clients. (Can you say the same about the business lawyers you use or most businesses in general?)

I mention all of this because we want the same success for you: a thriving enterprise and the confidence of a solid legal foundation. With the proper structure in place, you're ready to build the business of your dreams. The formula is simple but powerful—take care of home first, then you can dutifully help others.

We look forward to partnering with you in the future or giving you a push in the right direction. Between working *in* your business all day and *on* your business all night, it's safe to say you have enough on your plate. Let us take care of the fine print.

From the bottom of my heart, thank you for reading my very first book. I hope the conversational tone (and lack of boring structure and legalese that too many lawyers think make them sound smart) offers some comfort and ideas for improvement. After all, a business is like a tree—it's either growing or dying. There is no in-between.

Protecting the economy one business at a time,

Brett

Reviews

"A refreshingly candid look at the downfalls of so many companies and how easy it is to avoid those danger zones. Brett Trembly helps you navigate what they are and how to stay in front of the problems with short and to the point chapters that help you understand the issues and know how to protect your company."
Kristen David
The Kristen David, Upleveling Your Business

"As a valuation professional, I have worked with business owners throughout my career, and the biggest danger zones are those blind spots where they "don't know what they don't know." I've also valued trademarks and contracts and can attest that these are very valuable intangible assets, so it is imperative to get these right. Brett Trembly does a great job in highlighting the danger zones so that business owners can protect their assets and their futures. Proactive planning is worth its

weight in gold. An easy, practical, and valuable read."
Dave Bookbinder
author of *The New ROI: Return on Individuals*
www.NewROI.com

"First things first, if this book is intended for everyday business owners and laymen, it's such a success."
Jessica Faroy
Editor

"A great primer on what one needs to do to avoid pitfalls in starting and running a business. A must-read for any entrepreneur."
Matthew Weiss
Writer/Director of *Man In Red Bandana*

"This book is the candid conversation EVERY BUSINESS OWNER needs to read!"
Joel Gandara
Entrepreneur's Coach
www.JoelGandara.com

Foreword

Let's get something straight, right out of the gate: this book is immensely valuable and may save business owners a shocking amount of time, money, and stress. I know this because I learned many of its lessons the hard way.

I used to be one of those entrepreneurs who relied on resources like LegalZoom and business owner friends as my "attorneys." I'd go online to google answers to legal questions and download contract templates, aiming to save money. I was an eternal optimist who thought that *legal troubles wouldn't happen to me.*

I didn't realize how much this misconception would cost me in the long run.

In 2012, right after my first business had found its feet and was succeeding, I was hit with a frivolous class-action labor lawsuit. I had always done my best to take care of my employees, so I was shocked, angry, and hurt. I marshaled my resources to fight the claim and eventually won; a judge dismissed it. But along the way, I spent about a quarter of a million dollars, suffered untold stress, and almost let my emotions over the issue destroy my business.

If I'd read this book—and especially if I'd had a team of legal strategists like the Trembly Law Firm in my corner before it happened—I could have avoided almost all of that. I never thought about the value of having attorneys that spoke my language and were there for me in a proactive way.

Over the following years, I ran into several other legal issues that were prevented by having the right "Danger zones" covered, including a trademark violation, two business sales, a new operating agreement, and partner disputes. All went smoothly, thanks to the proactive advice from my legal team. It felt like they were part of my Leadership Team in the company.

So, you can call me a convert—I'm no longer a "LegalZoom" entrepreneur.

I now know the value of having quality proactive legal advice in my corner. I've realized a direct, huge ROI from working with Trembly Law Firm. I've learned that every deal is unique, every contract should be customized and rock-solid, and excellent legal representation doesn't just deal with problems as they arise. It stops many of them in their tracks—or before they even happen.

I sincerely hope that you never encounter any legal troubles. But given that Small Business Administration research shows that 36%-53% of small businesses experience litigation yearly, and many more issues never make it to court, the odds are not great.

I now feel confident, safe, and protected with the Trembly Law Firm in my corner. I hope you take Brett Trembly's advice in this book—and find a legal team that can speak your language and gives you the same peace of mind they give me.

Cesar Quintero
The Profit Recipe
theprofitrecipe.com

Introduction

Business owners are the backbone of our economy, supplying more than half of the jobs in the United States. Typically, an employer's day consists of dealing with clients, managing employees, and monitoring overhead, payroll, and expenses—as well as putting out fires. It takes courage and relentlessness to be an entrepreneur, and it's easy to become overwhelmed and miss critical elements of running a great business.

Are your ownership documents up to date and in writing? Are you surrounding yourself with the right advisors? Have you officially secured your trademarks? Or, have you accidentally stepped into the Danger Zone? Not taking even the smallest measures can leave your business vulnerable to potential lawsuits and, in some cases, even company closure.

That's why our legal team at Trembly Law analyzed years of litigation data to identify the fifty most common areas threatening businesses today. We broke these down into five categories, which we call the *Danger Zones*. Each chapter in this book illuminates threats, shares cautionary tales, and provides proactive advice designed to help you stay out of court and in business— where you belong.

Thanks to the current state of affairs, several well-intentioned but ultimately harmful laws, and unscrupulous contingency-based lawyers, employers are being attacked from all angles. Thankfully, there's a way to fight back, and by reading this short book written in plain English, you can start to gain back control and sleep well at night.

After reading this book, you should have a better understanding of the common employment pitfalls that await business owners, and how to protect yourself—and your business—in the future.

The First Danger Zone: Corporate Infrastructure

Many people go into business on a handshake, a promise, and a prayer. We've heard countless success stories that started in someone's garage, such as Amazon and Microsoft. Aside from their humble beginnings, these companies had something else in common—the inevitable struggle for equity, buyout, and, assuredly, ownership.

If you read the book *Accidental Billionaires* or watched the movie *The Social Network,* you know the "founders" of Facebook were embroiled in years of litigation because they lacked written documentation. Unfortunately, this shoot-first-and-ask-questions-later philosophy is all too common in business; most entrepreneurs simply don't take the time to put corporate documents in place to protect their business. They think, "Let's go into business and start making money, and we'll deal with it later. We're all friends here. I'm sure it will be fine."

Whether it's poorly drafted documents or lack of documents all together, weak infrastructure planning lands business owners in court. In these next pages, we'll discuss three areas to look out for: drafting operating or shareholder agreements, legally incorporating a business and constantly revising and drafting bylaws. Once you know which documents to put in place, you'll be sure to avoid common mistakes like CPA (Certified Public Accountant) reliance and revision failure.

The Time to "Get Legal Advice" is Before There's a Problem

Let's be honest, as long as the money is coming in, you normally don't stop to think about protecting yourself, your business, or your assets. You're simply too busy hustling every day. But in a business with multiple partners, problems arise when you rely on memory instead of officially signed documents— especially when everyone remembers the same event differently. Even with the best intentions, there are no truths, only versions thereof; and those versions can get very expensive, very quickly.

Perhaps more frustrating than neglecting to document ownership in writing, many budding entrepreneurs get poor legal advice. Sometimes, poorly drafted documents cause more heartache than no agreements at all.

Case Study: Revisions

We often hear, "Attorneys are too expensive," or, "We just didn't want to slow down and take the time to put all of our documents in place." Let me show you what happens when you don't "take the time."

Trembly Law Firm represents a client who started a business in the late '80s. For twenty-five years or so, business was swell.

Fortunately, the shareholders wrote up an agreement in the early 1990s. Unfortunately, it left a lot to be desired. For over twenty-five years, the three shareholders grew and managed an almost ten-million-dollar company. As the business continued to grow, no one revised the shareholders' agreement, drafted bylaws, or even organized annual meetings (these simple steps are crucial for every functioning business, comparatively speaking, they're not even very expensive). Verbal agreements were offered, some were accepted, and a few alleged corporate modifications were written via email. The business was moving fast, and so were the owners—especially the one with bad intentions.

It turns out that the third shareholder had been setting up an attempted corporate takeover for several years. He claimed to have requested and received over fifty percent of the company on a deal made via email, which led to a costly litigation case that has dragged on for years.

Let me just state that it is very hard to save a corporation that experiences fighting among shareholders. At that point, the business normally implodes. Everything you've worked for disappears because each side will fight to the bitter end. It's much easier to save a business from outside threats than to deal with internal strife.

In this case study, thankfully, we have a happy ending. Afraid of losing their business despite three decades of dedication and financial foundation, the two very honest shareholders reached a settlement with the third shareholder. (Without giving away too much detail, let's just say that the two shareholders hired good counsel!) What is there to learn from this situation? You can overcome the devastation and business wreckage of prolonged litigation by revising and drafting official documentation.

One last point to make—in our court system, you have to respect the golden rule: he who has the gold makes the rules. This rule isn't a fun reality, and it's not *always* true, but it usually is. The guys or gals doing the right thing, such as in our case study, don't always come out on top. This is even more reason to have your documents in order before you spend most of your working life building a company.

The Best Place to Start is at the Beginning

As I said earlier, the first Danger Zone is corporate infrastructure, and usually a lack thereof. If you are starting or thinking about starting a business, immediately consult someone to help you get your "stuff" together. It's not a pride thing, either. You don't know what you don't know. Fake-it-till-you-make-it may work in business, but not in litigation. If you're currently in business and thinking, "I'll handle it someday," that day is today. You must ensure that your documents are in place and your business is protected.

It's not always a lack of corporate infrastructure to be wary of; it's poor document drafting. Another huge and somehow largely unidentified problem for business owners occurs when Accountants play corporate business makers for their clients. With all due respect, CPAs lack a legal background. While your CPA should help you create a tax strategy, they should not incorporate your business nor select your legal entity.

At Trembly Law, we've come across business owners with years and years of experience who will confidently hand over a big black binder and say, "Here are my books." Usually, the binders are completely blank inside. The scenario typically plays out as such: Your CPA offers to incorporate your business, so they do... but only online. Then, they grab an Employer

Identification Number ("EIN") and order a fancy book with pre-printed "stock certificates" in a binder. Reasonably so, this makes the never-the-wiser business owner believe they have solid corporate documents. Again, we see this all the time. Dearest accountants, a note—stop it.

So what happens when business owners fight over ownership without corporate records? Time to look through tax returns and other circumstantial evidence. In these particular cases, business partners try to prove who owns what and who's in control. Once again, someone ends up in court, digging through Florida corporate statutes and trying to save the company.

Getting Everything Together

As far as your documents are concerned, a Limited Liability Company (LLC) is normally a great option, and, depending on your goals, so is a corporation. No matter the business structure, you must have your operating agreement or your shareholder agreement in place. If pursuing an LLC, draft an operating agreement; corporations, on the other hand, require a shareholder agreement. This is your business bible.

These agreements state who owns what, who's responsible for what, who's allowed to do what, and who isn't. Ultimately, these private documents function as legal guides to the ownership and decision-making structure of the business. It may not seem like a big deal and may even appear obvious, but things change, and so does memory. This is why it is essential to have everything in writing.

Before placing anything in writing, I'm often asked whether to file a partnership, an LLC, or an S Corp. For starters, an S Corp is not a legal entity. It's just one way a company can be taxed.

The default entity should be an LLC, and you should always register in your home state. We're asked about incorporating in Delaware often, but unless you're going to be a ten-million-dollar company, it's not worth the hassle.

If certain things are in place, you could also choose to file as a partnership or a corporation. My advice is to meet with your attorney and your CPA simultaneously as a team of people who can guide you. By getting everyone together in the same room, you can sleep well at night knowing you've done the absolute best thing for your company with the highest amount of protection available.

Key to Success Tip: Sunbiz[1]

Sunbiz is a very misunderstood part of the Florida government. Here, business owners can register and file an annual corporation report

---

[1] For our non-Florida readers, "Sunbiz" is the corollary to your home state's division of corporations where you register and file annual corporate reports.

with the Division of Corporations. Many business owners falsely believe that whoever's name appears on Sunbiz owns the company. It doesn't work that way. Sunbiz can be changed easily and without notice. It can also list you as a director, not an owner, a common trick of "veteran" corporate manipulators. For the most part, Sunbiz only exists to organize and display public records. Please don't rely only on Sunbiz. It provides virtually no protection.

Nutshell

Fighting over ownership is just one of the ways poor corporate documents can haunt you.

The bottom line is this: If you never took the time to draft a proper operating or shareholders agreement, and there is more than one owner, drop what you're doing and reach out today. If a lawyer prepared an agreement for you, but it has been so long that you're not sure where even to look, drop what you're doing and find it today. If your CPA played lawyer and "prepared" documents for you, drop what you're doing and reach out today. We've failed to completely protect a few businesses because they pushed back on "what is necessary," and we couldn't push back harder. We're not letting that happen again. Call today, and let's finalize your first Danger Zone—corporate infrastructure.

In the meantime, here are some questions to ask yourself:

- Do I have ownership documented in writing?
- Does it exclude emails, verbal agreements, or outdated documentation?
- Do I have a drafted and signed operating or shareholder agreement?
- Is my business filed as a partnership or corporation?
- Do I have bylaws in place?
- Are all my documents up to date?
- Were my documents drafted through legal counsel or a CPA?

The Second Danger Zone: Employment Matters

There's a lot to talk about when it comes to employment, and we can't cover it all in this book. But there are two areas posing a major threat to employers and causing a huge rise in lawsuits over the past few years: overtime (wage and hour) and discrimination actions. Avoiding these expensive lawsuits can be as easy as taking pointed preventative measures—having a time tracking system in place, correctly classifying employees and contractors, following employment handbooks, and drafting employment agreements.

A big revelation for business owners is that many of these lawsuits don't arise out of intentionality. Most owners think they're out of harm's way because they lack ill intent. The real danger is in not realizing what exposes a business to trouble.

It's important to take the time to educate yourself and create relationships with the right people to guide you through this Danger Zone. We understand the need for speed for our very fast-growing clients, the movers, and shakers who never have time. When trying to strike a deal or make a move, stopping to have your lawyer review documents delays the process – but it's a necessary delay.

Making sure you take time to dot your I's, cross your T's, and do everything by the book is important. In this chapter, we give you general advice on avoiding common traps and what type of documents to have in place in case avoidance isn't possible.

Are They an Employee or Independent Contractor?

Let's start by explaining the difference between an employee and an independent contractor. Many businesses want to hire employees and avoid the hassle of doing it the right way. To get around this, they try to pay employees as independent contractors. This can lead to costly overtime claims for the business. Listen, we get it. The rules are arduous, but let's not fret over what we can't change.

The main difference between an employee and an independent contractor is what's called dominion and control. If someone working for your company must show up at a certain time and leave at a certain time, ninety-nine times out of one hundred, they're an employee. If they have to dress a certain way, as in wear a uniform or follow company guidelines, they're most likely deemed an employee.

True independent contractors are just that—independent. They can come and go as they want, dress how they want, act how they want, and work from wherever they want so long as they carry out a contractual task. A typical example is hiring an information technician to fix a computer. The technician may come in and fix the computer for you or take the computer offsite; the technician may choose to do it at night or on the weekends. They were hired to complete the job, and even if that job must be completed by a certain time, they can do the task when they feel.

We often see the other end in construction or in-home healthcare. Some business hires are assigned projects or clients but are also required to wear a uniform, follow a delivery route, work or be available during certain hours, answer calls on a phone, etc. Those are all components that would lead a judge or jury to determine the person an employee.

In the delivery route scenario, if the worker has a right to refuse a job or can accept or reject delivery routes as they see fit, they *should be* deemed an independent contractor. If the delivery driver has a set schedule with no discretion on whether to accept a route, they will likely be found to be an employee. The easiest reference these days are Instacart employees. They can come and go as they choose and accept or reject deliveries or rides. They don't work for the grocery store; they work for themselves, as much or as little as they want.

The problem with misclassifying someone as an independent contractor is twofold. First, they can claim overtime (which we cover later), and second, you can be hit with years and years of back taxes. There's a proliferation of lawsuits for alleged overtime claims in South Florida, many of them by former employees alleging they worked more than forty hours a week for years but were paid flat rates as independent contractors and are therefore owed overtime. Needless to say, these lawsuits are not pretty or cheap.

Overtime Allegations

Even if you properly classify an employee, you will still get in legal trouble if they're working more than forty hours a week and not being paid overtime. Putting employees on salary (as opposed to hourly) pay and then believing they're not entitled to overtime is a classic mistake employers make. In some cases, you can indeed put someone on salary and have them work more than forty hours a week without overtime compensation, but only if they're paid a certain amount and are a "management-level" employee. This can only be done with employees with a high level of autonomy and decision-making power, such as restaurant managers, who often work sixty-hour weeks. Otherwise, forty hours a week is the limit without legally owing overtime.

Case Study: Time Tracking

Recently, Trembly Law handled—and won—an overtime allegation lawsuit. Here, the former employee claimed to have worked twenty additional hours a week for more than three years, looking for more than a six-figure payout. Our client, who had not been our client until the lawsuit started, did not have very good employment records. A common mistake among business owners is relying on hours of operation in place of a solid timekeeping system. It is important to note that even if a business is only open from 8 a.m. to 5 p.m., owners should still implement timesheets or other time tracking forms to protect against overtime allegations.

Without our client's exact records, we pieced the story together with testimonies and depositions. However, it was a lot like winning the battle and losing the war. Our client had to spend so much money on the litigation that the business ended up closing anyway. It was a long battle, which was ultimately too costly for the business owner.

I'm aware this seems like a lot of red tape and administration just to give people jobs, but it will save you a great deal of money if done the right way. If you can present a time log as evidence that an employee didn't work extra hours, you will have a very short case. Since you can fight off those claims, chances are you'll win on a motion dismissed or summary judgment. However, without time records, you're facing a presumption (a legal assumption the court must accept as true) that the employee did work those hours, and it becomes very timely (and costly) to rebut that presumption and prove otherwise.

You may be reading this and thinking, "Why am I reading so much about timecards? I'm a sophisticated business owner; this isn't why I read this book." You would be surprised at how many large and midsize businesses still forget to keep time records in hopes of creating an environment where people can come and go. These days we hear more and more about open workplaces, unlimited time off, and many other new developments in the corporate world, but we can avoid costly problems by doing something as simple as tracking our employees' time. It may be a pain, but it will be much less painful than getting slapped with an overtime claim.

Finally, have we mentioned that overtime claims could come with <u>personal liability</u> to the business owner? Yeah, you read that right. That's why we spent so much time on it in this book. Don't mess around.

Key to Success Tip: Time Sheets

There are many different types of sophisticated third-party apps – on ever your payroll company—that will help you track employee time. These apps monitor employees' location when they check-in and check-out via the GPS on their cell phones. Some people still use punch cards, where you clock in and clock out manually, and others use the good old-fashioned paper and pencil. Either is much better than nothing, but heed this important tip—you need to ensure the time log gets signed by the employee every week, or that log is self-serving evidence worth about as much as the paper it's printed on.

Employment Handbooks and Employment Agreements

This is not an either/or scenario; we prefer you have both employment agreements and signed employment handbooks as a regular part of your business. Again, more red tape. Again, very worth it.

Employment agreements can protect a business by defining the scope of employment, the rate of pay, and the type of employment (at-will or otherwise). The employer and the employee should sign employment agreements before the employee begins employment. When drafting an employment agreement, two important items to define are scope of work and pay. Though many of our clients skipped this step until they began working with us, it's never too late to get it in place.

There are certain things you should put into employment agreements and certain things you cannot put into employment agreements. For this, you'll need a professional—such as a business attorney. A typical agreement states the date of employment, the agreed-upon salary, receipt of the handbook, and many other provisions, such as non-competes or non-circumventions. Employment agreements should protect the business, but they also need to be reasonable to the employee and not long enough to scare them away.

Employment handbooks are important because they can help protect your company from certain types of discrimination claims. Believe it or not, it's better not to have employment handbooks than to have them and only selectively enforce them. Once you get more than five or six employees, you will want to have an employee handbook written, and you're going to want to enforce it.

The employment or team member handbook contains all the company rules you wouldn't put in an individual employment contract. It runs the gamut of everything you need to communicate business regulations: dress code, business hours, social media policies, time off, sick leave, potential protected items, proprietary information definitions, computer use and protocol, parking, and so on.

Once you put the rules down, it's important to stick to them. Not following your handbook can open you up to claims as well, such as discrimination (favoring certain employees or over others) or wrongful termination. The best practice is to put everything in writing and remain complicit across employee levels with enforcement. This means there can be different rules for management-level employees than for administrative employees, but not disparate rules amongst the classes.

Discrimination Allegations

Discrimination claims arise when an employee is fired and then alleges to have been discriminated against because of gender, race, or age, or otherwise treated differently from other employees. They also arise when there's different treatment among same class employees, whether it's management-level, executive-level, or staff-level employees. All of these items should be defined in the employee handbook, with a nicely written anti-discrimination policy.

Discrimination and overtime lawsuits are a rising trend in Florida, putting a lot of stress on business owners. Like overtime allegations, discrimination suits can be avoided with proper paperwork and consistent documentation, especially leave and termination policies. If your company doesn't have a severance agreement template (an agreement amongst the business and employee defining terms of separation and severance pay, if any), it needs to be created. Like the aforementioned agreements, a properly drafted severance agreement can save you a lot of time and a lot of money.

Termination Procedures

Employee termination becomes especially problematic when business owners do not follow equal procedures or federal rules and regulations. Let's say your company has a three-infraction rule (nicely spelled out in the Employment Handbook, of course). If you choose to fire an employee after the first infraction but others after the third, you're no longer consistently enforcing the rules across the same employee class. This leaves your business vulnerable to a discrimination claim.

In federal court, we've seen an increase in discrimination claims as attorneys convince fired employees to file discrimination lawsuits. Normally, defending against a lawsuit is so expensive that a business owner would rather cut a twenty-five-thousand-dollar check than spend three times as much on legal fees. It's very frustrating to get hit with one of these lawsuits; if you have a severance agreement, then you might be able to avoid the whole thing. If your company offers severance pay, ensure the employee signs off confirming they reviewed or got an attorney to review the agreement. This way, business owners avoid ex-employee lawsuits.

You can also hire outside help with terminations firing, such as a Human Resources (HR) company. Not many people know this is a service they offer.

Leave Policies

Aside from termination policies, some of the biggest mistakes are found in paid time off (PTO) and leave policies. Whether or not a company has written policies on time off, sick leave, bereavement leave, or maternity/paternity leave can play a huge role in discrimination charges.

Let's say you authorize six weeks of maternity leave. Without a policy in place, you forget and authorize four weeks of maternity leave the next time around. This can lead to a claim, and consistently enforcing rules is the only way to avoid it. Remember, the best policy is a written policy. Carefully drafting and following bereavement, maternal, and sick leave policies within employee handbooks set a precedent and help avoid potential discrimination allegations.

Key to Success Tip: EPLI

Here's a crucial tip I hope you heed: getting Employer Professional Liability Insurance (EPLI) can save you tens of thousands of dollars. If or when a former employee sues the company, this insurance coverage not only insures you for an award of damages, but it provides for cost and fee coverage for defending the claim. One of our clients was sued twice in one year for discrimination. Although we won both claims, the number of attorney's fees the defendant paid was just painful and had they had EPLI, they'd have a much fatter bank account right now.

You may be eligible for EPLI if you have an employee handbook and consistent standards. At Trembly Law, we tell all of our clients to please secure an EPLI policy and later help them gather the necessary documents. The insurance coverage is tough to get, but having your attorney's fees covered when an employee sues can make all the difference in the world.

Nutshell

Lawsuits against employers are rapidly growing out of control, especially in South Florida. Properly classifying employees, carefully documenting true independent contractors, utilizing employment agreements, and drafting and enforcing employment handbooks can all be classified as smart business ownership. It's not rocket science; it's prudence. You're working hard to grow your business and provide jobs, but don't leave yourself exposed while you're doing it. Ask yourself:

- Am I correctly classifying my employees and/or independent contractors?
- If my employees are on salary, are they entitled to overtime?
- Do I have a timekeeping system in place, or do I rely on business hours?
- Do I have signed employee agreements detailing the scope of work and pay, salary, date of employment, and other provisions?
- Do I have employee handbooks that address leave policies?
- Do I have and enforce an equal and proper termination procedure?
- Do offer severance (and require a signed severance agreement in exchange) to all employees leaving the company?
- Do I have EPLI coverage?
- Should I consider hiring a Human Resources company to handle agreements and termination?

The Third Danger Zone: Contracts and Lease Agreements

As I've previously noted, fighting amongst shareholders or business partners most often spells doom for the company. Third-party disputes, however, are normally a manageable nuisance and, some would say, a rite of passage in the business world.

Look, I get it. Contracts and agreements aren't sexy. Most people just want to talk about sales and marketing. We've tried to do our best to liven things up by telling some good war stories and giving real-life accounts. Contracts will never be particularly sexy, and there's no need to pretend otherwise. But you need them. You need them to be sound, solid, and to provide you with leverage. You need them to predict the future.

We're happy to do all those things for you. Just please, don't say you need one done by tomorrow! So let's dive in.

Let's Talk About Contracts, Baby

Contracts refer to any sort of vendor agreement with anyone supplying goods or services to your business. A commercial lease agreement is also a contract; it's a legally binding contract between a business owner and a landlord. With contracts and lease agreements, the most problematic areas are relocation, liens, termination, and zoning.

Commercial Litigation and Contracts

Commercial litigation involves two or more parties, ultimately fighting over money. Someone didn't get paid and isn't happy, someone had to pay, or refused to pay, and isn't happy, or some variation thereof. But it always involves parties dealing in commerce in some way, and more often than not, a contract is involved.

When dealing with third-party disputes, we always try to put our clients in the best possible position by creating great contracts and lease agreements pursuant to the latest development in contract law.

Contract law, so to speak, develops when a party sues another and a judge makes a ruling on a clause, or even a sentence, contained in a contract. The losing party appeals and an appellate court writes a fancy decision, which ends up guiding lawyers on how to write contracts. Books on contracts are hundreds of pages. Courses in law school are months long. Contract law is voluminous, to say the least. Don't you think it's important to get good help with your contracts?

Because this is a short book, we simply can't cover everything about contracts. But you deal with them every day. You have agreements with how you conduct business, and so does everyone else. The more money on the line and the more that money means to you, the more important it is to have a good contract.

Contracts boil down to containing one thing, as a good friend and mentor of mine is fond of saying: who is going to do what, by when. If you're expecting services and having to pay, you want those conditions met. If not, you want the best possible footing upon which to break the agreement and not pay. You want the tribunal that best suits you (both forum and venue). You might want attorneys' fees included or excluded for strategic reasons, and you might want other remedies included or excluded in writing. What you can put in a contract is almost limitless. (Let's just say that sometimes we get very creative.) But a contract is your best shot at creating your ideal scenario for what happens when the agreement is breached. Rushing through a contract or trying to get one done cheaply is often a terrible idea. As good lawyers are fond of saying, there's nothing more expensive than a cheap lawyer.

The different types of contracts are almost virtually limitless. But if you're reading this, you likely have a specific area of business or a trade that you're familiar with, and therefore you're interested in only a few types of contracts relevant to you. Have your contracts been reviewed regularly? Don't do business on a handshake. Yes, I know lawyers can be expensive, and we certainly don't believe in scare tactics as a method of gaining business, but there's a reason Miami-Dade County has the fourth busiest court system in the nation. You cannot trust people, and perhaps more importantly, you cannot trust their memories. Or your own. Get your agreements memorialized on paper, and if you want to protect your business, have your contracts done by a great lawyer that will give you ultimate leverage in a sticky situation. It's often better not to use the court system to enforce the contract, but having the option always gives you the upper hand.

The Devil's in the Lease-tails

Having your commercial lease agreement reviewed by a real estate broker is helpful, but attorneys are able to look out for problematic clauses unknown to companies or agents.

Many areas in the commercial leasing space can get clients in legal and financial trouble. If a business owner is not careful, landlords can take advantage. Commercial eviction actions are not just limited to situations where a savvy landlord takes advantage of an unsuspecting new business owner by utilizing a tricky clause in a bad lease agreement. Often, the lessee (business moving into the commercial space) doesn't take the time to thoroughly review the lease agreement in the first place. Once more, they think, "I'll just deal with it later."

Case Study: Relocation Clause

One crucial area to review is the relocation clause. Trembly Law once had a client sign a retail space lease without having us review it— can you imagine that?! Later, a mall representative approached them, saying a new, more recognizable tenant would occupy their space. As a consequence, our client was moved to the back of the mall.

Once we were pulled in, we took a look at the existing lease only to find out that, sure enough, the mall had the right to relocate our client. Because there was a very clear contractual agreement, the client's only choice was to delay and stall the relocation with a lawsuit that they would eventually not win. That's an expensive endeavor and ultimately not worth it. To make a long story short, the business eventually shut down because the new location was as unprofitable as we initially imagined.

Case Study: Termination Clause

Another one of our clients in the restaurant space ran into a terrible dispute after their business shut down. Arguably, our client was set up to fail by the landlord from day one. The landlord reduced the number of parking spaces necessary for the restaurant to survive, and on the day of the grand opening, the plumbing overflowed into their space. Talk about a sh!%y deal!

Obviously unhappy, our client demanded to get out of the lease, and the landlord "let" them... verbally. Without securing a release in writing, they packed up and left, only to be hit with a lawsuit a few months later, requesting three years of rent for hundreds of thousands of dollars.

After being hired by the client to defend the lawsuit, in one of those rare moments right out of a movie, we were able to find a smoking gun. That rarely happens, but it happened here, and it was enough to force a good settlement for our clients after several years of expensive litigation where both parties emotionally dug in.

Again, don't forget about the golden rule. Landlords by and large have much larger war chests than tenants. If our clients had the money, armed with the smoking gun, we could have rolled the dice at trial. Not only would we have won the case, but we would have secured our attorneys 'fees (which would have been a nice payday for a young and ambitious lawyer with very few clients at the time). However, the client has to foot the bill for the case, and, alas, you must always do what's best for the client, which in this case, it was to settle. In retrospect, it's easy to say, "We should have fought that case until the end," but it's always easy to spend other people's money. (Make sure your lawyer isn't happy to do this to you!)

Key to Success Tip: Space Negotiations

One of the worst things that can happen to a business owner is to have a physical space that limits growth. We've seen many of our clients' businesses grow, but their physical space limits that growth. One tip we give is negotiating for the right to be given more space in the lease or, if the building can't provide you with more space, to be let out of the lease altogether. If you want more square footage but it is unavailable, and you have pre-negotiated for more space in the event you need it, you can maneuver your way out of the lease with your landlord. In this case, negotiation can save you quite a bit of money.

Let Me Out!

When your time is up, take advantage of it. If your lease agreement is up for renewal, you don't want to miss out on notifying your landlord that you're opting out. If you're planning to opt-out, or even exploring to opt-out of your lease, most contracts have automatic renewals, which can really frustrate a business owner. Once you miss the deadline, you're locked in for another term. Notify the landlord early, then use that notice to negotiate a better deal.

Case Study: Equipment/Property Liens

In yet another messy situation, one of our clients signed a lease agreement that, if breached, gave the landlord a lien on all the restaurant's kitchen equipment and furniture. This meant that the landlord held a right to keep possession of our clients' property in case of default. Imagine— you not only lost your business but all the expensive kitchen equipment as well. That's about as bad as it gets.

With regards to negotiating this lease, there weren't enough chefs in the kitchen. Pun intended. They should have requested an expert's help.

Alas, our clients (not our clients at the time) moved out of their space overnight and took their equipment with them, which landed them in some hot water later on. Our clients needed to sell the kitchen equipment to pay off debt, but legally speaking, they signed away the rights to the equipment.

This is a sticky situation to be in. The argument for including the lien in the lease is to help the landlord offset damages. But do you think a landlord, entrusted with the possession and sale of the equipment to offset rent, is ever going to work hard to get top dollar? Of course not, because they know you're on the hook for the rest of the unpaid rent anyway. Worst of all? Most, if not all, lease agreements require a personal guarantee. This is just another nightmare scenario that most people don't stop to think about when starting a business.

Nutshell

If you haven't noticed already, I could spend all day telling stories about the consequences of overlooked clauses in lease agreements. Contracts and lease agreements are not fun, sexy topics, but neither is getting sued or losing your business. It won't ever be sexy to read and review contracts and documents. Have you noticed the common theme in the short examples above? The tenants waited until there was a dispute to find legal help instead of working with an attorney ahead of time. Once again, preventative and proactive legal work is always a fraction of the cost of reactive legal work.

Yes, getting lawyers involved slows the process a bit and will cost you some upfront money, but it will be pennies compared to litigation costs. It may cost you more now, but it'll be a lot more valuable at the end of the day.

To recap, let's go over the key questions in contracts and lease agreements:

- Does my contract say who is going to do what, by when?
- Are my contracts current and being reviewed regularly?
- Have I had my attorney look at my lease agreement?
- Is there a relocation or termination clause in my lease agreement? If not, can I secure a release in writing?
- Is there an equipment or property lean on my lease agreement?
- Does my lease agreement negotiate for more space? If not, can I secure lease termination?
- Does my lease agreement include automatic renewals and a notice period?
- Do I have a venue selection clause in my commercial contract convenient to me, and have I considered an alternative dispute resolution forum?

The Fourth Danger Zone: Intellectual Property

At this point, almost everyone knows how to identify a trademark. A trademark is an officially registered "mark" consisting of a logo, words, or both in commerce. It works by protecting the word or image in a certain classification (such as restaurants, professional services, manufacturing, etc.) against the incorrect use of that image or logo, set of words, or combination of words and logo. There are many classifications for trademarks. If you own a bakery, a trademark will protect you against another bakery using your name, image, or logo. However, you would not be able to prevent a sporting line from using the same name.

While most people think of Coca-Cola or McDonalds when discussing trademarks, it's just as important for business owners to secure their marks. **I cannot say this loudly enough: get your trademarks, people!!!**

I scream this message because we've seen too many business owners suffer on account of poor trademark precaution. Business owners who have been operating for years, building a brand, only to receive a cease and desist letter and waste years of blood, sweat, and tears. Potential lawsuits, or worse, business closure and limitation, are possible to avoid with a trademark.

In this chapter, we'll go over the most common consequences-- litigation costs, business closure, limitation, and renaming-- and misconceptions-- thinking it's too late, relying on the Division of Corporations, and not trademarking across categories and products.

Pre-Plan and Save!

No, that's not our attempt at an energetic infomercial pitch. It's deadly accurate. Registering for a trademark can cost as little as just over a thousand dollars. Litigating over the trademark, you neglected to register will cost tens of thousands.

To avoid that situation, we recommend filing for trademark registration as soon as you first use the mark—as soon as you put the mark on a website, in a marketing email, or hang the sign outside your door. Once you get your trademark, you're in the driver's seat to enforce your rights, and preventing someone else from using the mark can be as simple as sending a cease and desist letter.

Just Because It's "Yours" Doesn't Mean It's Safe

One of the worst things that can happen to your business is not trademarking the name or logo and then having a competitor come in and use it. You've worked for years to build a reputation, only for someone else to swoop in and register the trademark first. This can not only cause a lot of confusion in the marketplace; it could potentially put you out of business.

The reasoning behind trademark protection in the first place is to prevent marketplace confusion. Would you like it if you were drinking a "Coca-Cola" that was made by a different company? You wouldn't trust what was actually in the can, which is clearly problematic. Would we like it if another law firm down the street started using the name "Trembly Law Firm" to attract customers with our hard-earned goodwill? Of course not.

Unfortunately, while many business owners understand the need to protect their name, they also believe that because they have registered the business on Sunbiz (or your own state's Division of Corporations website), the name itself is protected. This is problematic for three reasons. First, a business can always register a fictitious name similar or identical to yours. Second, registering within your state doesn't give you protection elsewhere. Third, trademarks provide federal protection, meaning another business can register your name first and then prevent you from using it within your state.

I'm not going to apologize for repeating myself again: stop messing around and get your trademarks! Otherwise, gut-wrenching things can happen.

Case Study: Love Thy Neighbor

A few years back, we got a call from a business owner who had a competitor move next door to him and started a company with the same name. The intent was to confuse—the exact scenario that trademark laws are designed to help prevent. After ten years of building his business, the owner was up in arms. Worse yet, the owner decided to deal with the situation the "old-fashioned way." (We are not sure exactly what that meant, and because the potential client decided not to engage our services, we'll never know.) The proper thing to do would have been to rush to file for a trademark on the business name.

Registering for a trademark is just the first step. The public is then put on notice that the mark is being registered, giving someone else who may be using the mark the opportunity to challenge the registration. Now, the second company could have decided to fight against the registration, but you deal with it when it comes. This can ultimately turn into a litigation battle with a multitude of possible outcomes, including an agreement for concurrent use. The litigation can be expensive, and, as always, it's exponentially more costly than simply registering in the first place.

In this case, the gentleman that called had been in business longer, and had he registered first, would have likely prevailed. Bottom line, if you file, you can protect yourself. If you don't, you're at risk.

It's Never Too Late

I was asked just the other day, "I've been in business twenty years; why should I trademark now?" Let's use a common scenario as an illustration: you've been in business for five years in Florida. All of a sudden, a business in Georgia opens, uses your same business name and files a federal trademark registration. If you don't challenge the trademark and the Georgia company is successful in their registration, it may prevent you from doing business in your state! Sometimes, you can continue running your business because you were the *first to use* the mark, but you'll most assuredly be prevented from expanding to other states using that name.

Wherever you are, whether you've been in business for a year or thirty, you should trademark your name and logo at once. Of course, you should first investigate whether or not you can trademark. Afterward, you'll want to move as fast as possible.

I was also asked recently, "If someone else trademarks the name first, even though you've been in business for many years, could they force you to change your name?"

The short answer is, "Possibly, because we've seen it before." There are a lot of factors the examiner will consider, meaning there aren't any "bright-line" rules for us to say "yes" or "no" emphatically. Sometimes you can continue to use the marks you've held for some time, and other times, you can't.

It's simply not worth building a business that's unprotected. And it's especially not worth spending attorney's fees in federal court over something that can cost as little as a few thousand dollars to protect. Don't want someone else to force you to change your name? Get the damn trademark. Have we been emphatic enough?

What Else Can I Register and Protect?

We're often asked about creating a trademark for a business name and logo. If you're serious about business, you'll do both, even though it costs just a bit more. And, if your enterprise crosses into multiple categories, you'll register in those categories as well. Yes, the cost can add up, but it's worth it.

That said, building your intellectual property portfolio doesn't need to stop there. Many sophisticated companies secure trademarks not only for the name and the logo of the business but also for every product line they roll out. For example, it's not enough for Ford to own a trademark on the name "Ford" when it comes to automobile manufacturing and sales; they need to register trademarks for every line of vehicle they come out with, such as the F150. Another example is a beverage manufacturing company or local brewery. Whenever you come out with a new beer, it's prudent to secure a trademark for that line, lest a big company swoop in and intentionally create a competing (and confusing) brand.

Key to Success Tip: International Protection

Seek out trademark protection at once, but also give very good consideration to international protection. If you have any possibility of expanding or doing something in another country, such as selling a product on Amazon, you should protect yourself internationally as well as domestically. Overall, you want to investigate all three levels: state protection, federal protection, and international protection.

International trademark protection can really change your business trajectory in terms of business growth. Without strong protection, a competitor can claim you're infringing on their rights and have you shut down, even if it's temporary. We see this a lot in Amazon wars: someone in another country will replicate a product, leave consumers with a replica from another seller rather than the original product, and then claim they were first to market. When you're dealing with a country like China, it's hard to enforce your rights. At the same time, treaties require most countries to recognize international trademark registration. At the very least, give yourself the most protection available, even if it's not perfect, because it's better to have a fighting chance.

Nutshell

Securing a trademark for a business name and logo seems daunting to the everyday business owner, but it's not. But by now, we've learned that trademark infringement isn't just limited to big corporations like Coca-Cola or Ford. You, the local coffee shop owner, sushi restaurant, or online drop shipper, you also need your trademark.

We've seen small businesses face the consequences of this Danger Zone too often. If someone with your name or a similar logo opens up and files first, you can be forced to change your name. Even if you're first to operate, failure to secure a trademark will prevent you from expanding if another business registers first. And let's not forget that a competitor may even shut down your business or replicate your products if you lack international protection.

If you're still on the fence about trademarking your name and logo, remember that whether you've been in business for ten years or ten days, it's never too late to file a trademark. Keep these questions in mind when trying to assure you're protected against possible trademark complications:

- Have I used my company mark in my marketing emails, website, posters, etc.?
- Have I thoroughly researched whether or not my company name and logo are already trademarked?
- Have I trademarked my business name and logo?
- Have I registered my business on a state division of corporation website, like Sunbiz, and not with the United States Patent and Trademark Office?
- Does my business cross into multiple categories, and have I registered my trademark within them?
- Do I need to secure a trademark for every product I roll out?
- Have I looked into state, federal, and international protection?

- Is my product vulnerable to replication that may require an international trademark?

The Fifth Danger Zone: Regulatory Compliance

Often under-reported and ignored, lack of regulatory compliance (local, state, and federal) can get a lot of companies in legal hot water. And while many areas of non-compliance won't be disastrous because you can work through them, there are two major areas I want to touch upon that are devastating businesses across the land. The first is the proliferation of lawsuits under the Americans with Disabilities Act (ADA), including both alleged violations of physical and online space, and the second is a new and developing area of litigating under a law called the Telephone Consumer Protection Act (TCPA). Luckily, dodging ADA and TCPA lawsuits is possible by taking precautionary measures, which we'll cover in this chapter.

ADA Lawsuits

Under the ADA, a claim will allege that your premises—or website—are not accessible for someone with a disability. In South Florida, there are hundreds of lawsuits filed against building owners every day. These lawsuits are a total nuisance—they are expensive to defend, and, even when settled, the defendant gets stuck with chipping in for "fees" (which I'll explain further below). These lawsuits make a variety of (usually unsubstantiated) claims: a counter is too high, a toilet paper roll is not exactly where it's supposed to be, a handrail is a little bit off, there are too few disability parking spaces, the ramp isn't at the correct angle, or the parking spaces are too narrow. With regards to the website issues, which we discuss more thoroughly below, the allegation is that a sight-impaired person cannot fairly and equally navigate your website.

These are a lot of what seem like rather benign or, more importantly, easily repairable problems. But instead of providing notice to the business owner and allowing them to correct the deficiency (our argument for how enforcement of the law should be handled), you—the business owner—now have to hire an attorney to defend a lawsuit in federal court, potentially pay to fix all the alleged ADA violations, and pay the plaintiff's attorney.

The law itself—the Americans with Disabilities Act—is, of course, a well-intentioned law. What's affecting business owners is the abuse of the law by a new line of unscrupulous attorneys, the new "ambulance chasers" of the legal field. The lawsuits are often unsubstantiated, but it costs the business owner at least fifty thousand dollars just to prove their case because they're in federal court. The far more common outcome results in the business owner settling for a lot less. But even settling and fixing the premises can cost upwards of twenty thousand dollars, no small fee for small business owners.

The prevailing party's attorney's fees clause—which states that if any allegations in the lawsuit are correct, the defendants (usually the business owner and/or landlord) will have to pay at least a portion of the plaintiff's attorney's fees—doesn't make defending these lawsuits easy. This usually drives up the cost enough so that employers and landlords choose to settle and stroke a check, even though they may prevail in the lawsuit.[2]

The takeaway here is that you should proactively inspect your property now and fix any ADA violations, minor or otherwise. Just as we've been preaching this entire book, such proactive measures cost pennies compared to reactive

---

[2] I am on record in the Daily Business Review calling these lawsuits legal extortion.

measures. A few thousand dollars now can save you tens of thousands of dollars later.

Online ADA Lawsuits

The scary thing is that ADA lawsuits have moved from the physical world to the online world. A wave of lawsuits is being filed against anyone and everyone who has a website that's not ADA "compliant." If this is the first time you've heard of this issue, you may be thinking, "How can my website not be ADA compliant?"

If your website doesn't include auditory signals for visually impaired consumers, then you could be in violation of the ADA and face a lawsuit. The real problem here is that there are no defined rules on what makes a website ADA "compliant." That's right—because this is a new area of law and litigation, there's virtually no way to guarantee your website is 100% ADA accessible. So, if a company comes along and makes the claim that they can "fix" your website and guarantee ADA compliance, make sure you get that guarantee in writing. Vague claims to "fix" your website issues only lead to more frustration for the business owner.

One easy step to protect against an online ADA violation is installing a widget on your website that can provide audio access to the seeing impaired. Of course, there are other steps to take. To combat this further abuse of the ADA, at Trembly Law, we've created a website for business owners to check their website's current code in place to help with ADA compliance: **app.sitecompliance.com/tremblylaw**. Again, there's no way to guarantee compliance, but you can at least do your best to mitigate your exposure by working with the right company.

As far as the ADA goes, whether online or not, inspect the premises and website before you're hit with a lawsuit. Or, if it's too late and you're served with a lawsuit, there are a lot of preliminary steps to avoid further exposure. Please call us right away and get your website checked out.

TCPA Lawsuits

The TCPA is a federal law extended to text messages. The law provides damages to the person receiving the text, paid by the company sending the text. The maximum penalty is one thousand five hundred dollars per occurrence, which doesn't sound like a reason to file for bankruptcy. Think again—because the lawsuit will be filed in federal court as a class action on behalf of *all* text message recipients, discovery normally reveals thousands of text messages and potential damages of millions of dollars, plus attorney's fees.

When you visit Home Depot, Pizza Hut, or even Party City, do you notice that they ask for your phone number? Why do they do this? The truth is, the more information they have on you, the more ways they can market to you (or sell your information). When you give these large businesses your phone number, you usually do so while simultaneously agreeing to be solicited via text. Somewhere along the way, small businesses decided to engage in text message marketing, but this grand idea can have disastrous consequences.

Text message marketing has been increasing in popularity, mostly driven by opportunistic marketing companies who have no idea that what they're pitching is potentially in violation of the TCPA. Restaurants are a common victim of this pitch. Let's say that hundreds of customers are coming in and out of your restaurant daily, and you start collecting their phone numbers as part of the check-out process. Because the phone numbers were given voluntarily, the restaurant believes that they have a right to text these customers. Unfortunately, if the restaurant owner hands over the phone numbers to a marketing company, who then mass texts the list, it will likely result in a costly violation.

Ask Before You Text

As a business owner, if you pick up your phone and start sending a text to your clients, it's okay. You may annoy some of them, but that's your decision as a business owner. The violation of the TCPA only applies to mass "Robotexts" via a machine.

Other requirements must be met under the TCPA. For example, if you pay attention, you'll probably notice an opt-out clause the next time you get a text from a company. This is required by the TCPA (and likely other ordinances or regulations). While you need to have an opt-out to send a marketing-based text message, just including the opt-out still doesn't guarantee compliance with the TCPA. The first and most important requirement for sending mass texts is seeking and receiving affirmative permission before you text.

While you are allowed to send texts to your customers one at a time, it's better to ask for affirmative permission to text them. Opportunistic lawyers are too ready to sue a business they think has deep pockets for violation of the TCPA. These lawyers are advertising more and more, seeking anyone who received unsolicited texts to potentially file a class-action lawsuit. Yes, it's unfortunate, but for now, it's the law. Better to comply. Bottom line, think before you text (AKA seek expertise).

Case Study: Hold the Line

We recently defended a large client sued under the TCPA. In this case, the plaintiff sought a judgment of more than five million dollars. The allegations were that our client illegally sent thousands of text messages, without permission, to hundreds of unsuspecting persons from an automatic texting machine (the "Robo-dialer").

We dug into the case and fought hard, and we were able to defeat most of the allegations. (The plaintiff also made some mistakes, which can't be made in federal court, and we pounced.)

After a lot of effort (and legal fees), we forced a complete walk away, and our client was off the hook. Of course, we cannot guarantee results like this, but hiring the right firm also makes a huge difference. Even better than prevailing in court, though, is never getting sued in the first place. The money our clients spent on legal fees was at least ten times the amount it would have cost them to investigate the law in the first place properly. Had they been a member of our proactive general counsel program, we like to think we would have caught this ahead of time. Hopefully, someone will read this book, and we'll save them gobs of money and even more heartache. I will be thrilled to receive that email someday!

Key to Success Tip: Avoid New Marketing Companies

Most of the time, marketing companies claim they have the latest technology and pitch a business owner with this new idea.

It's tempting to think, "Hey, I have ten thousand customers in my database. With just one click of a button, I can send a text message offering a discount on the brunch buffet." Even more tempting is thinking about how many people will come in for brunch that day. It makes a lot of sense, but it's not allowed under the law, no matter what the upstart marketing company owned by your kid's friend tells you.

I would strongly recommend business owners avoid texting consumers altogether unless they can assure their business is in compliance and has insurance that shields them against any types of claims. If those two things aren't in place, then I would steer clear. It's not worth the risk.

Nutshell

The TCPA and ADA are two well-intentioned federal laws that leave misinformed business owners vulnerable. Whether it's a result of ruthless lawyers or marketing guerillas, defending against these lawsuits gets costly— and so does the settlement. If you're unsure whether or not your business is vulnerable to an ADA or TCPA lawsuit, ask yourself:

- Have I inspected my property for ADA violations and fixed any issues?
- Have I determined if my website is ADA accessible by first utilizing the Trembly Law site compliance tool?
- If I text my consumers, have I sought and received affirmative permission to text?
- Am I sending mass text messages with automatic machines, such as Robo-dialers?

- Am I soliciting or releasing cellular information to marketing companies?

Circumventing the Danger Zones in Seven Steps: How to Protect Your Business

Phew! Now you're sufficiently scared of anything and everything. Not so fast. At Trembly Law, we follow a seven-step system to protect your business from potential Danger Zones designed to keep you out of court. While you may be thinking, "Here comes the sales pitch," we unapologetically recommend that our clients protect themselves. It's not that hard to address nearly everything discussed in the previous chapters, and we'll show you how. By doing so, you'll be better protected than 90% of business owners out there.

Step One: Develop a Proven Hiring System

As previously reviewed in this book, many employment complications come from a poor hiring and recruiting system. Do you do background checks? Do you have multiple interviews? Do you check references? Chances are you intend to, but other things get in the way.

With a structured, detailed interview system, performed the same way every time and pursuant to vetted HR guidelines, you'll avoid most of the exposure your counterparts won't. At the interview stage, handwritten notes should not be kept, every person should be asked the same interview questions, and there should be multiple people in the interview. This prevents a lot of hiring discrimination claims.

Once hired, you should constantly review your accountability chart to ensure you have the right people on your team. We recommend working with a business coach in this regard. You should also have detailed notes in each employee's HR files and always follow your employment handbook's discipline review system. We have lots of other suggestions, but these are the main ones for this short book. Bottom line: maintain excellent records.

Step Two: Utilize Employment-Related Contracts

Employment agreements, independent contractor agreements, severance agreements, employment handbooks, non-compete agreements, the list goes on. Get your legal ducks in a row on your employment-related agreements, and you'll sleep easy at night. Putting employment agreements, handbooks, and a consistent enforcement system in place will do wonders for your business and heavily protect you against the aforementioned discrimination lawsuits, or put you in a great position to successfully defend yourself.

Here's where step one also comes in—the more resources you pour into hiring the right people, the fewer problems you'll have, and the happier you'll be. From the hiring system flows the rest of the business. If you have willing, happy employees signing employment agreements, reading a robust, healthy employment handbook, and following a very detailed infraction enforcement system, you'll have healthy severance protection when the time comes.

Step Three: Get Insurance

Earlier, I mentioned EPLI. If you're sued by an employee for discrimination and/or overtime claims, for the most part (depending on what the policy says), the insurance company must pay your legal fees for the defense. This is a completely non-self-serving tip: if you have this insurance, you'll receive insurance-provided attorneys for your defense, and they'll pay for your settlement (again, depending on the policy). If you don't have this insurance, you're going to need to hire a skilled team of legal defense counsel (ahem, us) and pay a lot more money. I would rather you have the coverage and stay in business, working with a similar firm or us to stay in compliance and out of court, rather than hope you don't get sued and have to pay legal fees.

Step Four: Get a Legal Diagnostic and Develop a Game Plan

I use the following analogy often—getting a legal diagnostic is a lot like routine car maintenance. If your car is running, but you haven't looked under the hood in several years, you have no idea if you're safe or only a few miles away from disaster while going eighty miles per hour on the freeway. You could blow a gasket, run out of power steering or brake fluid, or the engine could catch on fire. Not likely, but possible. This is also why cars have dashboards—these are trouble indicators warning you when something is about to go wrong.

But what trouble indicators does your business have in place when one of the Danger Zones is about to strike? Let's face it—we don't all have beautiful business dashboards with red and yellow flashing indicators when something is about to go wrong.

That's why we suggest annual legal diagnostics to see what's "under the hood." This is what we do with our general counsel clients—at least the ones that take our advice! We go through all fifty-plus exposure points and triage what we need to address. Sometimes it's not bad news at all, and other times we avoid a head-on collision.

We invite you to go to our website, www.TremblyLaw.com/DangerZones, and fill out our personalized survey to determine your exposure level, for free. Think of it as a way of knowing what's under the hood before you break down and have to fix something rather expensive that could have been avoided.

Once the diagnostic has been performed and triaged the necessary items to address in your business, we create a timeline and a game plan and then get to work. Rather straightforward— let's fix the flashing red lights first, then fine-tune what's holding you back. By giving specific, intentional attention to your business's inner-working, you'll have the sweetest ride on the road.

Step Five: Hold Regular Meetings with Your Business Development Teams

Once we arrive at the fifth step, we start making recommendations for better business operations and compliance. We suggest working with a "development team" that includes a CPA, a business coach, and an insurance broker because you don't need to limit your professional advice to just your attorneys. And yes, we've been hard on CPA's in this book, but there are lots of good ones out there to work with. When you're operating at an extremely high frequency, you're likely meeting with your business team once per quarter, ensuring your car is now a well-oiled machine. This is an expense, and it takes time, but it sure is less expensive than waiting until the whole engine blows.

Step Six: Engage in Profit First (Financial Prudence)

We are currently the only Profit First™ certified business law firm in the state of Florida. While most firms say they really care about their clients, we back up that claim with action. We help many of our clients implement Profit First™ in their businesses because, as the saying goes, "Broke business owners can't help anyone." Additionally, if you're barely skating by with slim margins year after year, I know you're miserable, and life is too short to be miserable.

It gets really frustrating when you go through all of the heartache and stress of starting your own business, paying the bills, trying to market and sell, filling orders, and end up paying everyone except yourself. It puts you in a place that's not fun to be in. Look at it this way—don't your hard-working employees deserve to know they work at a financially prudent and stable company?

Okay, you get it, and you agree. But what is Profit First™, and why are you discussing it? We have developed a custom Profit First™ system at Trembly Law that helps our clients implement Profit First™ into their businesses. It's the same system that helped us navigate the recent COVID-19 pandemic without having to fire a single person, and a few months into the pandemic, getting back into growth mode while most law firms floundered. Profit First is about financial responsibility, not greed. We'd love to have a conversation with you about the system and see if we can help. In our experience, most business owners neglect their financial systems AND pay themselves last. This is a risky proposition, and we're doing our part to help root out this financial imprudence where it most exists—with small business owners that ordinarily lack the time, and resources, to properly address this concern, strange as that may sound.

Step Seven: Follow an Operating System

The final step in our business plan is developing an operating system, that is, a proven system for running your team. This entails hiring a coach or proven program to develop a lot of the processes we've reviewed: hiring, team management, financial management and growth, and team communication.

As you're growing, it's very important not to reinvent the wheel. A lot of businesses get stuck on the hamster wheel of working really hard when most often, we have to work smart. Savvy business owners realize that working *on* the business instead of *in* the business is the only way to get out of the rat race once and for all. But still, how do you know you're doing the right things? That's where expert help comes in. There are a lot of great resources that we're able to recommend to help our clients keep growing their business, non-legally speaking.

Again, Trembly Law doesn't just believe in providing legal solutions. We believe in providing business resources as we partner with our clients to help each other grow. We're part of your team, and if we're to take our mission of *protecting the economy one business at a time* seriously, we need to do more for you than just answer the phone when the proverbial you-know-what hits the fan.

Conclusion

If there's one thing to take away from this book, it's this—taking proactive and tedious measures to protect your business costs pennies compared to litigation and settlement checks. Of course, trademarking and overtime pay isn't free. But neither are the lawsuits over ownership, trademark rights, contracts, and lease agreements, discrimination and overtime allegations, and ADA and TCPA non-compliance your business may be vulnerable to.

Hopefully, by now, these five Danger Zones seem a lot less daunting to deal with. With the help of the aforementioned steps, protecting a business from *avoidable* lawsuits can be as easy as drafting and revising ownership agreements, documenting and enforcing HR protocol, reviewing lease agreements, securing trademarks, and inspecting your property, website, and telemarketing. Not all lawsuits are avoidable, however, and in that case, you want the leverage on your side via carefully crafted legal agreements.

But aside from a solid legal foundation, I hope you take away nuggets of wisdom that don't just apply to the judicial system. Don't forget that it's *never* too late to get an employment agreement or trademark in place or to reduce that oral amendment to your operating agreement to writing. And especially, *do not* replace legal advice by trusting marketing companies or CPAs.

Business owners shouldn't have to make the same mistakes twice. Even better, they should learn from the mistakes of others. With these tools, tips, and tales from the trenches, I sincerely hope your business has fewer things to worry about after you put down this book and take action.

Don't forget to take the Danger Zone quiz for yourself at www.tremblylaw.com/DangerZones.

Best of luck on your journey. *You* are the engine that helps our economy run, and we humbly thank you for your hard work.

About the Author

Brett Trembly is the Founder of Trembly Law Firm, a franchise, business, employment defense, and litigation law firm in Miami, Florida. From one attorney in 2011, the firm has grown to ten attorneys and twenty-five employees at the time of publication and was just named in the prestigious Inc. 5,000 list. Trembly Law represents some of the largest businesses in the eastern United States, as well as many medium and small local businesses. All clients are equally important, as the firm's mission is to "protect the economy one business at a time."

Brett grew up near Albuquerque, New Mexico. In 2005, he moved to Miami to attend the University of Miami School of Law. He lives in Palmetto Bay, Florida, with his wife and three children: Liv (age eight), Ritter (age five), and Bentley (age two).

In the South Florida legal community, Brett has served as President of the South Miami Kendall Bar Association and as Vice-Chair of the Florida Bar 11th Circuit Grievance Committee. He also volunteers on the Florida Bar Young Lawyers Division Mentoring Program, the Dade County Bar Association's Rainmakers Committee, and annually for Miami-Dade County's Ethical Governance Day. Brett was named a Super Lawyers "Rising Star" in Florida for the past five years and, yes, this is true, was a participant on American Ninja Warrior.

Regarding his philanthropic and business involvement, Brett is strongly committed to leadership and giving back, having served as President of the Rotary Club of South Miami, President of a BNI. Chapter, and Vice-President of the Rotary Foundation of South Miami, Inc. He has also served as Director of the Palmetto Bay Business Association and has also been a Board Member of the Gentlemen's Journal. Brett is actively involved in the Pinecrest Business Association and the Entrepreneurs' Organization and was recently selected to sit on the Board of the Nicklaus Children's Hospital Foundation.

The Trembly Law Firm also hosts (when not interrupted by COVID) an annual Charity Domino Tournament to benefit local charitable organizations.

Made in the USA
Coppell, TX
02 May 2021

54860997R00046